Phonics and Word Study

Continental Press

ISBN 978-0-8454-3854-1

Table of Contents

Write the missing consonant in each picture name below. Use the letters *b, f, h, j, k, l, m, n, p, r, t, v, w,* and *y.*

____ane   ____elmet   ____ater   ____eather

sanda____   doorkno____   crow____   magne____

fou____teen   com____ass   ca____el   coo____ies

The paragraphs below contain some incomplete words. Use the consonants listed at the top of the page to complete those words.

In the ____orld of sports, the Olympics are unique. They were begu____ near____y three thousand ____ears ago in a____cient Greece. The ____irst game was a simple foo____ ____ace over a dis____ance of a____out two ____undred ____ards. It was ____eld ____ear the ____own of Olympia. A____ter the first game, i____ was decided ____o ____old the games e____ery fourth year. They ____ere called an Olympiad. The Olympics ____ecame ____ery ____opular, and ____ore co____tests were added. Then a Roman e____peror pu____ an end to the____.

A Frenchman organized the first ____odern Olympics. In 1896, ____ine countries e____tered the games. They ____ave ____een held nearly eve____y fou____ years since then. Today almost two hundre____ countries are i____volved. Ath____etes co____pete in all ____inds of sports from ____oxing to ____ong ____umping to ____ater ____olo. The modern games are held in or near diffe____ent ci____ies throughou____ the world.

In some words, two or three consonants come together, and their sounds are blended. These are called *consonant blends.*

The most common blends are listed in the box at the right. They can be found at the beginning, middle, or end of words.

Consonant Blends				
br	pr	gl	sk	scr
cr	tr	pl	sw	spl
dr	bl	st	tw	spr
fr	cl	sp	sm	str
gr	fl	sc	sn	squ

Complete each word below by adding one of the above blends to the letters shown.

____ ____ank   ____ ____out   ____ ____eech   ____ ____itch

____ ____ank   ____ ____ ____out   ____ ____ ____eech   ____ ____itch

____ ____ace   ____ ____im   ____ ____ash   ____ ____eam

____ ____ace   ____ ____im   ____ ____ash   ____ ____ ____eam

____ ____ace   ____ ____im   ____ ____ ____ash   ____ ____ ____eam

The paragraphs below contain some incomplete words. Use the blends listed at the top of the page to complete those words.

Did you ever a____ ____ yourself where dinosaurs and other ____ ____ehistoric animals lived? Was it a faraway ____ ____ace? Actually, these ____ ____eat bea____ ____s roamed many parts of the world, in____ ____uding the United States. A discovery in Colorado may ____ ____ove to be the bones of the largest animal that ever lived. This ____ ____ ____endid dinosaur ____ ____ood 60 feet tall. The leafy tops of ____ ____ees were a tasty ____ ____ack for the 80-ton animal. Its length ____ ____ ____ead 80 feet between the tip of its nose and its tail.

Scientists have also found remains in North Dakota. Fifty million years ago, the land there was as ____ ____ampy and ____ ____opical as the Ever____ ____ades. Fifteen-foot long ____ ____ocodiles lived there. So did ____ ____all alligators. Many of the bones found in North Dakota are ____ ____ ____ange. One animal was like a modern ____ ____apping turtle. Besides animals such as lizards and ____ ____ogs, the remains of ____ ____owers and trees have also been found.

In some words, two consonants come together and form one special sound. This sound is different from either of the two individual consonant sounds. These are called *consonant digraphs.* The most common ones are listed in the box at the right.

Consonant Digraphs

ch	ng	th
ck	sh	wh

Complete each word below by adding one of the above digraphs to the letters shown.

___ ___in   ___ ___at   ___ ___op   ___ ___eat

___ ___in   ___ ___at   ___ ___op   ___ ___eat

lo___ ___   sma___ ___   la___ ___   hu___ ___

lo___ ___   sma___ ___   la___ ___   hu___ ___

The paragraphs below contain some incomplete words. Use the digraphs listed at the top of the page to complete those words.

One day the movi_____ van pulled up to our house on Forest Street. I felt sad. _____at house was like a friend to me. I knew every cra_____ and corner in it. In the new house, _____ough, ea_____ of us _____ildren would have our own bedroom.

After the move, every_____ing seemed fine. Our new house was in perfect _____ape. There were bu_____es in front of it and a garden in the ba_____. Nothi_____ at all seemed wro_____.

But _____en strange _____ings began to happen. One night _____en we came home, the clo_____ was broken and on the kitchen floor. It had been ha_____ing on the wall. It couldn't have fallen and broken from _____ere it was. Late one night, my dad heard somethi_____. He jumped out of bed and found the door open, but no one was _____ere. He climbed back into bed, but then he heard _____ispers. Again he _____ecked the house. No one was there. Dad _____inks it was just someone talking _____ile they walked up the street. Maybe it was. I'm not so certain, _____ough. _____at do you _____ink?

Consonant Digraphs   5

Some consonants have more than one sound.

c   /k/ c̲ot, /s/ c̲ider, /sh/ with *i* anc̲ient
ch   /ch/ c̲heese, /k/ ac̲he, /sh/ mac̲hine
d   /d/ d̲ance, /j/ with *u* gra̲dual, with *g* bri̲dge
g   /g/ g̲ift, /j/ g̲em
s   /s/ s̲ea, /z/ hers̲, /sh/ with *u* s̲ure, /zh/ with *u* pleas̲ure, with *i* televis̲ion
t   /t/ t̲ime, /ch/ with *u* nat̲ure, with *i* quest̲ion, /sh/ with *i* nat̲ion
th   /th/ bo̲th, /th/ smoo̲th
x   /ks/ box̲, /gz/ ex̲ample

On the first line after each word below, write the symbol that represents the sound of the underlined letter or letters. On the second line, write the key word from above that contains the same sound.

1. car**g**o _____ _____

2. vi**si**on _____ _____

3. para**ch**ute _____ _____

4. perple**x** _____ _____

5. **c**elery _____ _____

6. i**ss**ue _____ _____

7. **ch**orus _____ _____

8. **th**ere _____ _____

9. **d**efeat _____ _____

10. ri**g**id _____ _____

11. cea**s**e _____ _____

12. e**x**haust _____ _____

13. occa**si**on _____ _____

14. sugge**st**ion _____ _____

15. **s**ugar _____ _____

16. **th**eater _____ _____

17. solu**ti**on _____ _____

18. pou**ch** _____ _____

19. **c**orral _____ _____

20. s**ch**edule _____ _____

21. e**x**plode _____ _____

22. musta**ch**e _____ _____

23. **t**ype _____ _____

24. es**p**ecially _____ _____

25. knowle**dg**e _____ _____

26. serie**s** _____ _____

27. indivi**du**al _____ _____

28. **ch**aracter _____ _____

29. so**c**ial _____ _____

30. ven**tu**re _____ _____

Long and short vowel sounds often have more than one spelling. Notice that the following words have the same vowel sound but different spellings.

three   p**ea**ch   monk**ey**   ch**ie**f

Complete each sentence below by writing on the line one of the words at the right of the sentence. The word should include the vowel sound given at the end of the sentence.

1. Dad spends a great deal of time working at his

   desk in the /e/ _____.   office   kitchen   den

2. If you do not wash the spilled /u/ _____

   off the floor, ants will be everywhere.   crumbs   juice   food

3. The mysterious words carved on the rocks

   /a/ _____ the scientists.   baffled   confused   amazed

4. Brian likes the oatmeal with /ā/ _____,

   but Kim Lee does not.   fruit   raisins   bananas

5. The job of a lawyer is to /ī/ _____

   people of their legal rights.   advise   tell   inform

6. Carry that bucket carefully, or the water will

   /o/ _____ over the side.   slosh   spill   go

7. Jane gave Antonia a /i/ _____,

   but she still couldn't answer the riddle.   clue   sign   hint

8. The woman's /ō/ _____ billowed

   and snapped in the wind.   cape   cloak   blouse

9. When painting a room, it's always best to

   start with the /ē/ _____. center   ceiling   walls

Long and Short Vowels   **7**

The sound of long **a** /ā/ is represented by these five spelling patterns.

ea—g<u>rea</u>t   ai—<u>bai</u>t   ey—th<u>ey</u>   ay—cl<u>ay</u>   ei—fr<u>ei</u>ght

Long **a** /ā/ is also represented by another spelling pattern.

a/consonant/silent e—*game, plate*

In each group of words below, circle the two words with the long /ā/ sound.

1. brain	flea	flake	6. prey	saint	peak
2. mane	clay	sneak	7. eighty	flank	faith
3. thread	drain	relay	8. tray	raid	crease
4. weight	mat	painful	9. scrape	plaid	delay
5. shriek	praise	vein	10. trailer	lay	release

Complete each sentence below with a word that has the long **a** /ā/ sound. Use words from the word box.

WORD BOX

harness	hail	cane	beat	ray	small
stray	graze	reins	veils	traitor	stains
scarf	break	steak	spy	meat	eat

1. When Beth pulled on the _____, the horse slowed to a trot.

2. Who do you think will _____ the Olympic swimming record?

3. The old man picked up his _____ and walked slowly out the door.

4. When sheep _____, they chew the grass off close to the roots.

5. A sad, _____ dog crawled onto our porch during the storm.

6. How can I remove these ink _____ from my hands?

7. A single _____ of sunlight poured through the hole in the roof.

8. Benedict Arnold was accused of being a _____ during the Revolution.

9. Would you like your _____ rare, medium, or well-done?

10. In some countries, women wear _____ to cover their faces.

The sound of long **e** /ē/ is represented by these seven spelling patterns.

e—h<u>e</u>   ea—t<u>ea</u>m   ei—c<u>ei</u>ling   y—cop<u>y</u>
ee—b<u>ee</u>f   ie—f<u>ie</u>ld   ey—donk<u>ey</u>

In each group of words below, circle the two words with the long **e** /ē/ sound.

1. obey   we   valley
2. grease   great   chief
3. breed   vein   key
4. peach   search   shriek
5. beetle   pulley   dread

6. relieve   reins   receive
7. cheat   steed   sweat
8. parsley   bully   apply
9. deny   naughty flee
10. grief   weapon   beaten

Complete the paragraphs below with words that have the long **e** /ē/ sound. Use words from the word box.

WORD BOX

train	she	apes	lonely	short	grew
sad	believed	teach	success	ideas	monkeys
succeed	achievement	sentences	brief	eagerly	increased

For years, scientists have tried to _____ animals to

communicate. Dr. Roger Fouts was one of the first to _____.

He knew that _____ can use their hands as people can.

Fouts _____ that chimps could learn sign language.

In 1966, Fouts began working with a chimp named Washoe. In just a

_____ time, Washoe was using simple signs. Soon

_____ was putting them together to express

_____. In time her vocabulary _____ to

over two hundred signs. It was a remarkable _____. And

when Washoe had a baby chimp, she _____ began showing

the signs to the infant. In only eight days, it made its first sign!

The sound of long i /ī/ is represented by these three spelling patterns.

ie—l*ie*   igh—s*igh*t   y—sk*y*

Long i /ī/ is also represented by another spelling pattern.

i/consonant/silent e—*ride, size*

In each group of words below, circle the two words with the long i /ī/ sound.

1.	fig	sly	divide	6.	slice	captive	lightness
2.	pastime	lie	grief	7.	magnify	thrive	gravity
3.	deny	envy	survive	8.	fling	hive	pry
4.	delight	horrify	celery	9.	strive	sigh	ditch
5.	brief	bike	slight	10.	midnight	active	supply

On the line in front of each definition below, write a word that has the long i /ī/ sound. Use words from the word box.

WORD BOX

hike	reply	pie	terrify	right	scare
correct	necktie	reptile	lime	shirt	lizard
thigh	march	apply	hip	lemon	answer

_____   1. A dessert often filled with fruit

_____   2. To respond to a question

_____   3. Proper

_____   4. The upper part of the leg

_____   5. To put in a request for something

_____   6. An article of clothing

_____   7. To make afraid

_____   8. A juicy, sour fruit

_____   9. A long walk

_____   10. A cold-blooded animal with scales

The sound of long **o** /ō/ is represented by these five spelling patterns.

o—*her*o   oe—*toe*   oa—*roast*   ow—*grown*   ou—*dough*

Long **o** /ō/ is also represented by another spelling pattern.

o/consonant/silent e—*note, stove*

In each group of words below, circle the two words with the long **o** /ō/ sound.

1. tiptoe	canoe	cloak	6. sole	shove	sorrow
2. howdy	solo	sparrow	7. moose	loan	vote
3. none	lone	soak	8. froze	goal	broad
4. prowl	soul	hoe	9. foam	mow	meow
5. glove	globe	toast	10. grouch	boulder	cargo

Complete the paragraphs below with words that have the long **o** /ō/ sound. Use words from the word box.

WORD BOX

neared	foe	enemy	chased	left	piece
crows	drove	tar	approached	loaf	elbow
echo	sound	robins	although	rose	coal

John James Audubon _____ from his warm bed

_____ dawn was still an hour away. Gathering pencils, paper,

and a _____ of bread, he headed for the woods. Soon he

spotted a pair of _____. He quietly _____ the

birds. Then, settling on the ground, Audubon leaned on one

_____ and began to draw. He captured every detail, even the

gleam of their glossy feathers, as black as _____. Suddenly the

big black birds spotted a fox. Cawing, they attacked their

_____. With flapping wings, they _____ it

away. Then the birds were gone. Only the _____ of their

cries remained.

Each of these vowel sounds is represented by more than one spelling.

/ū/—p_u_pil, f_ew_, c_u_b_e_   /ü/—t_oo_, s_ou_p, ch_ew_, s_ui_t, cl_ue_, fl_u_t_e_

The letters _oo_ also have the sound of /u̇/ in b_oo_k.

In each group of words below, circle the two words with the same vowel sound. Use only those vowel spellings listed above.

1. crook   broom   brook   6. toothpick   childhood   firewood
2. group   grouch   juice   7. perfume   preview   salute
3. stew   sew   due   8. cruise   harpoon   biscuit
4. pursue   foul   youth   9. blood   doom   shrewd
5. include   refuse   musician   10. community   prune   confusion

Complete each sentence below by writing one of the words given below the sentence. The word should include the vowel sound /ū/, /ü/, or /u̇/.

1. Amish farmers still use teams of _____ to plow their fields.
        horses   hounds   dogs   mules

2. Clouds of smoke rose out from under the _____ of the car.
        tires   hood   trunk   door

3. An ugly _____ showed where the baseball had struck Gail's leg.
        cut   mark   bruise   scar

4. An article about sunken treasure appeared in the last _____ of this magazine.
        issue   copy   chapter   section

5. Try not to lose the tiny _____ that holds your glasses together.
        nail   bolt   nut   screw

6. In some parts of the U.S., a _____ is called a mountain lion.
        panther   jaguar   cougar   leopard

7. Greg sent for a _____ about solar energy.
        booklet   magazine   report   publication

8. At rodeos, the bucking bull bursts out of a _____ .
        chute   corral   gate   ring

9. This recipe calls for a _____ of butter.
        pound   cup   cube   pat

A single vowel followed by *r* is neither long nor short. The *r* gives the vowel before it a different sound. When *or* follows *w*, it also has the sound heard in *work*.

ar	er	ir	or	ur
da<u>r</u>k	t<u>er</u>m	th<u>ir</u>d	n<u>or</u>th	h<u>ur</u>t
			w<u>or</u>se	

The spelling *ear* has three sounds: y<u>ear</u>   w<u>ear</u>   <u>earn</u>

Underline the correct name below each picture.

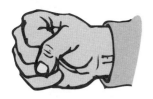

fist   first

mark   mask

lurk   lunch

held   herd

beard   bead

peas   pear

wool   world

peak   pearl

Read the paragraph below. On each line, write one of the words given below it.

Have you ever seen a shooting _____? The best time to
(star, stack)

_____ this _____ event is on a
(observe, object)   (remarkable, remainder)

_____, _____ winter night. Shooting stars
(clear, clean)   (dark, deck)

are better _____ meteors. These lumps of rock and metal are
(carved, called)

fragments of comets that _____ around the sun. When they
(whirl, while)

come too close to the _____, they _____ in
(each, earth)   (burn, bunk)

the atmosphere. All you see is a fiery _____.
(tear, trail)

In some words, two vowels in the same syllable form a special sound. It is made by gliding from the sound of the first vowel to the sound of the second. The two vowels together are called a *diphthong*. The most common ones are represented by the spellings *ou*, *ow*, *oi*, and *oy*.

/ou/ <u>ou</u>t, n<u>ow</u>   /oi/ c<u>oi</u>n, t<u>oy</u>

In each sentence below, underline the word or words containing one of the above diphthongs. Then above the word, write the symbol that represents the sound of that diphthong.

1. I read *The Grouchy Ladybug* aloud to my brother.

2. The judges' choice astounded the audience.

3. How does that man avoid paying taxes?

4. Mario hoisted the huge flounder into the boat.

5. Erin raised her eyebrows and lowered her voice.

6. Oysters and clams are the starfish's favorite prey.

7. Quickly the sheriff and his helpers surrounded the outlaw.

8. Each of the king's handkerchiefs was embroidered with a tiny crown.

The vowel spelling *ou* has more than one sound.

/ō/ th<u>ou</u>gh   /ô/ b<u>ou</u>ght   /ü/ gr<u>ou</u>p   /u/ y<u>ou</u>ng   /ou/ sc<u>ou</u>t

In each group of words below, circle the two words with the same vowel sound.

1. fought	doubt	ought	5. double	enough	sprout
2. bought	you	soup	6. brought	rough	thought
3. southern	noun	touch	7. tough	pounce	snout
4. dough	though	route	8. cougar	ouch	youth

The vowel spelling *ea* has more than one sound.

/ē/ m**ea**l   /ā/ st**ea**k   /e/ br**ea**d

In the paragraph below, underline each word with the vowel spelling *ea.* Then above the word, write the symbol that represents its sound.

The automobile has meant much to America. For a long time it was a source of fast, cheap transportation. In recent times, however, a great deal has changed. Gasoline supplies have lessened, and prices have been on a steady increase. With energy in today's headlines, the United States may be ready to look back. A vehicle powered by steam was invented in 1769. An electric car was already running in the late 1890s. But almost from the start, electric and steam cars had a bleak future. Old notions may provide useful weapons, however. They may give us an energy break by defeating today's fuel problems.

On the line in front of each definition below, write the correct underlined word from the paragraph above.

_____   1. Regular; unchanging

_____   2. The invisible gas into which heated water changes

_____   3. Not costly; inexpensive

_____   4. Means of fighting against something

_____   5. Prepared

_____   6. The words in dark print at the top of newspaper articles

_____   7. Large in amount

_____   8. A gain; growth

_____   9. Dreary; cheerless

The following single vowels and vowel combinations sometimes have the same sound. This sound is represented by the symbol /ô/.

/ô/	/ô/	/ô/	/ô/	/ô/
talk	force	cause	claw	thought

Circle each word below that contains the /ô/ sound. Then underline the letters that stand for the sound. Use only those vowels listed above.

1. bought
2. most
3. round
4. brought
5. rock
6. sidewalk
7. young
8. taught
9. group

10. ought
11. awful
12. salt
13. fought
14. sawmill
15. hawk
16. scout
17. ghost
18. cautious

19. chalk
20. stalk
21. thoughtful
22. haunt
23. foster
24. cougar
25. loft
26. shawl
27. awkward

28. audience
29. somersault
30. glory
31. caw
32. ignore
33. thaw
34. sauce
35. scorch
36. launch

In each sentence below, circle the two words with the sound /ô/. Use only those vowels and vowel combinations listed at the top of the page.

1. Nick filled the stalk of raw celery with cream cheese.

2. The author thought her book should sell a million copies.

3. The two brothers fought over the last piece of sausage.

4. Hawks are common in the northern part of the state.

5. Walk down the corridor and wait in the last room.

6. Mice gnawed through the wiring that opens the bank vault.

7. Addison cautiously approached the hornets' nest.

8. The bones of a dinosaur with horrible long teeth were found near here.

9. At dawn the sky was filled with glorious streamers of color.

10. The scientist wrote the formula on the chalkboard.

Spellings for /ô/—al, o, au, aw, and ou

The letters *w* and *y* may represent a vowel sound or a consonant sound. When *w* and *y* are at the beginning of syllables, they are consonants.

watch

yarn

When *w* follows *o*, *a*, or *e* in the same syllable, it is a vowel.

crown

claw

screw

When *y* is within a syllable or at the end of a syllable, it is a vowel. The vowel *y* can have three sounds.

/ī/ *fly*

/ē/ *puppy*

/i/ *cymbals*

On the line in front of each word below, write *V* if the underlined letter is a vowel or *C* if it is a consonant. If the *y* is a vowel, also write ī, ē, or i.

_____ 1. <u>w</u>aken

_____ 2. cre<u>w</u>

_____ 3. m<u>y</u>th

_____ 4. <u>y</u>ou'd

_____ 5. sl<u>y</u>

_____ 6. meo<u>w</u>

_____ 7. outla<u>w</u>

_____ 8. firefl<u>y</u>

_____ 9. ca<u>w</u>

_____ 10. rh<u>y</u>me

_____ 11. d<u>y</u>namite

_____ 12. eas<u>t</u>ward

_____ 13. activit<u>y</u>

_____ 14. <u>y</u>ank

_____ 15. satisf<u>y</u>

_____ 16. <u>y</u>elp

_____ 17. fa<u>w</u>n

_____ 18. <u>y</u>outh

_____ 19. boundar<u>y</u>

_____ 20. s<u>y</u>stem

_____ 21. sco<u>w</u>

_____ 22. <u>w</u>edge

_____ 23. <u>w</u>ept

_____ 24. rh<u>y</u>thm

_____ 25. elbo<u>w</u>

_____ 26. <u>y</u>earling

_____ 27. t<u>y</u>pe

_____ 28. <u>w</u>asp

_____ 29. intervie<u>w</u>

_____ 30. vo<u>w</u>

_____ 31. appl<u>y</u>

_____ 32. bulk<u>y</u>

_____ 33. <u>w</u>eapon

_____ 34. shre<u>w</u>d

_____ 35. ph<u>y</u>sical

_____ 36. pr<u>y</u>

In each row, circle the three words that contain the same vowel sound.

1. count   country   crowd   shore   trout   bowl

2. breeze   dream   view   brief   wealth   weigh

3. scour   score   tower   storm   loud   door

4. flow   flower   bone   groan   knot   rough

5. shut   hurt   crumb   cruise   trouble   count

6. claim   clam   cattle   trap   stare   salt

7. bright   child   twin   swirl   style   moist

8. blue   club   shoe   shout   crumb   who

9. now   noise   boys   scroll   fruit   point

10. bread   step   seal   term   end   sheet

11. cook   crow   school   scout   good   put

12. crib   trim   climb   field   quilt   dirt

13. class   chase   raise   stay   spare   chart

14. part   pair   farmer   place   grasp   charge

15. copper   dog   goggles   hot   corn   toe

Many words look alike except for a few letters.

bugle—bulge   *hurtle—hustle*

Complete each sentence with one of the words below the line.

1. As the sun became hotter, _____ rolled down my face.
   (sweet, sweat)

2. Mark wore dark glasses to _____ himself.
   (disguise, disgust)

3. Keira and her _____ ate at the Seafront Restaurant.
   (niece, nice)

4. An _____ is comfortable both on land and in water.
   (otter, other)

5. The expert declared that the painting was a _____.
   (fake, fate)

6. All animals must have oxygen to _____.
   (exit, exist)

7. Millions of mosquitoes lay their eggs in the still water of the _____.
   (march, marsh)

8. Listen to the loud _____ of the riders on the roller coaster.
   (shrieks, shrinks)

9. Many people like to _____ coins.
   (collect, correct)

10. We must _____ the boat with a tarp before winter comes.
    (color, cover)

11. The total is wrong because I made a mistake in _____.
    (edition, addition)

12. Eric likes to _____ in hockey and soccer games.
    (compete, complete)

The same vowel pattern in different words usually has the same sound, as *ai* in *maid, paid,* and *raid.* But sometimes the same vowel pattern has a different sound, as *ai* in *said.*

In each group of words below, cross out the word that has a different vowel sound. Then circle the symbol that stands for the vowel sound in the remaining two words.

/ō/	/ū/	**1.** shoe	toe	hoe	
/u/	/ō/	**2.** hose	whose	those	
/ī/	/ē/	**3.** dine	mine	machine	
/o/	/ō/	**4.** broad	road	load	
/ō/	/ū/	**5.** stone	done	bone	
/ē/	/ī/	**6.** give	hive	dive	
/ī/	/ā/	**7.** afraid	braid	plaid	
/u/	/ō/	**8.** dome	come	home	
/ā/	/a/	**9.** gave	have	shave	
/ō/	/ü/	**10.** to	so	go	
/ē/	/e/	**11.** seen	been	screen	
/ā/	/ē/	**12.** key	they	monkey	
/ī/	/ē/	**13.** try	country	apply	
/ou/	/ô/	**14.** loud	soup	shout	
/ā/	/ē/	**15.** pear	leaf	dream	

Each syllable in a word contains one vowel sound. To find out the number of syllables in a word, count the number of vowel sounds that are heard.

Below each word, write the number that tells how many syllables are heard in the word.

hammer   octopus   crib   guitar   binoculars

_____   _____   _____   _____   _____

Decide how many syllables are heard in each word in the word box.
Then write the words on the correct lines.

WORD BOX

volcano	leopard	social	determination	gasoline
diet	curiosity	variety	volunteer	organization
hike	extreme	nuisance	crease	heroic
magnet	similar	bracelet	tragedy	revolution
gratitude	obedient	triangle	reptile	appreciation
warehouse	goal	emergency	merchandise	antelope

ONE SYLLABLE

_____

_____

_____

TWO SYLLABLES

_____

_____

_____

_____

_____

_____

_____

THREE SYLLABLES

_____

_____

_____

_____

_____

_____

_____

_____

_____

FOUR SYLLABLES

_____

_____

_____

_____

FIVE SYLLABLES

_____

_____

_____

1 If a word contains a double consonant, divide **between** the double consonant.

fun | nel

2 If two unlike consonants come between two vowels, divide **between** the consonants.

hor | net

3 If a consonant comes between two vowels and the first vowel is short, divide **after** the consonant.

sal | ad

4 If a consonant comes between two vowels and the first vowel is long, divide **before** the consonant.

ra | zor

5 If a word ends in *le* and a consonant comes **before** *le,* divide before the consonant.

cra | dle

6 If two vowels come together in a word and each vowel stands for one sound, divide **between** the vowels.

li | on

On the line in front of each word below, write the number of the sentence above that tells how the word is divided. (Sometimes more than one number can be used.) Then divide the word into syllables.

_____ 1. willow
_____ 2. timid
_____ 3. poet
_____ 4. whittle
_____ 5. cotton
_____ 6. anvil
_____ 7. license
_____ 8. social
_____ 9. clover
_____ 10. normal
_____ 11. fever

_____ 12. volume
_____ 13. missile
_____ 14. climate
_____ 15. ginger
_____ 16. elbow
_____ 17. rascal
_____ 18. maple
_____ 19. filter
_____ 20. raven
_____ 21. dial
_____ 22. linen

_____ 23. rumble
_____ 24. brier
_____ 25. cable
_____ 26. labor
_____ 27. granite
_____ 28. perfume
_____ 29. meow
_____ 30. passage
_____ 31. armor
_____ 32. puppet
_____ 33. vivid

_____ 34. fumble
_____ 35. noble
_____ 36. otter
_____ 37. petal
_____ 38. corral
_____ 39. topic
_____ 40. witness
_____ 41. plastic
_____ 42. shimmer
_____ 43. bugle
_____ 44. riddle

1 Words that contain a consonant blend or a consonant digraph are usually not divided between the letters that make up the blend or digraph.

ma | chine   hy | drant

2 If a prefix or a suffix is added to a word, it usually forms a separate syllable.

fore | leg   art | ist

3 In a compound word, divide betwen the words that make up the compound word.

rail | road

On the first line in front of each definition below, write the correct word from the word box in syllables. On the second line, write the number of the sentence above that tells how the word is divided. (Sometimes more than one number can be used.)

WORD BOX

sickness	smother	repay	unsafe	describe	backbone
employ	doghouse	highland	messy	peaceful	suitcase

_____ _____ **1.** The spine

_____ _____ **2.** To keep air from something

_____ _____ **3.** Not neat

_____ _____ **4.** An unhealthy condition

_____ _____ **5.** To give back money owed

_____ _____ **6.** To pay for work done

_____ _____ **7.** To write or tell about something

_____ _____ **8.** The countryside far above sea level

_____ _____ **9.** A piece of luggage

_____ _____ **10.** Dangerous

The examples in each box show the different ways of dividing words into syllables. Divide the words in each group into syllables. On the line in front of each word, write the number of the box that shows how it is divided. (Sometimes more than one number can be used.)

1 Double consonants—*wil l low*	**4** Long vowel/consonant/vowel—*tu l lip*
2 Unlike consonants—*gin l ger*	**5** Consonant before *le*—*spar l kle*
3 Short vowel/consonant/vowel—*tal l ent*	**6** Between two vowels—*po l et*

_____ 1. dragon

_____ 2. cruel

_____ 3. radish

_____ 4. motel

_____ 5. butler

_____ 6. mammal

_____ 7. legal

_____ 8. attic

_____ 9. pepper

_____ 10. real

_____ 11. trial

_____ 12. motor

_____ 13. serpent

_____ 14. beetle

_____ 15. modest

_____ 16. stampede

_____ 17. talent

_____ 18. triumph

_____ 19. tennis

_____ 20. survive

_____ 21. baffle

7 Blend—*pil l grim* Digraph—*buck l et*	**8** Prefix—*re l pay* Suffix—*greed l y*	**9** Compound word—*row l boat*

_____ 1. untie

_____ 2. touchdown

_____ 3. hamster

_____ 4. scrapbook

_____ 5. playful

_____ 6. horseshoe

_____ 7. eardrum

_____ 8. unkind

_____ 9. reread

_____ 10. program

_____ 11. unroll

_____ 12. disgrace

_____ 13. smokestack

_____ 14. harmless

_____ 15. neglect

_____ 16. catcher

_____ 17. displease

_____ 18. eyesight

_____ 19. stillness

_____ 20. misspell

_____ 21. worship

_____ 22. flagpole

_____ 23. faithful

_____ 24. painter

If a word has more than one syllable, one of the syllables is usually stressed more than the others. This is shown by placing an accent mark (´) next to the syllable with the most stress.

let´tuce   *ca noe´*   *a´pri cot*   *mes´sen ger*   *pa ja´mas*

Decide which syllable in each word in the word box has the most stress. Write the word in syllables in the correct column below the box. Put an accent mark where it belongs.

WORD BOX

fan tas tic	sal ar y	pi o neer	voy age
ne glect	mir a cle	weap on	ap ply
ex plode	ca reer	ob vi ous	in ter rupt
im age	sub ma rine	vol un teer	di a gram
nui sance	sus pi cious	a ban don	tor pe do

TWO-SYLLABLE WORDS

Accent on First Syllable   **Accent on Second Syllable**

_____   _____

_____   _____

_____   _____

_____   _____

THREE-SYLLABLE WORDS

Accent on First Syllable   **Accent on Second Syllable**   **Accent on Third Syllable**

_____   _____   _____

_____   _____   _____

_____   _____   _____

_____   _____   _____

In words with more than one syllable, often more than one syllable is stressed. This is shown by placing a dark accent mark (ˊ) after the syllable with the most stress. A light accent mark (ˊ) is placed after the syllable which is also stressed but not as much.

hamburger
hamˊburgˊer

eyebrow
eyeˊbrowˊ

Each word below is divided into syllables. Put a dark accent mark (ˊ) after the syllable with the most stress. Put a light accent mark (ˊ) after the syllable which is also stressed but not as much.

1. ex pla na tion
2. lum ber jack
3. loud speak er
4. al li ga tor
5. guar an tee
6. mil i tar y
7. sub way
8. in vi ta tion

9. com bi na tion
10. reg u la tion
11. round up
12. in ter na tion al
13. bath tub
14. black smith
15. cel e bra tion
16. e vap o rate

17. man u fac ture
18. in di vid u al
19. rep u ta tion
20. com mu ni ca tion
21. co co nut
22. moun tain side
23. team mate
24. sat is fac tion

After each word below, write numbers to tell how many syllables it has, which syllable has the primary accent, and which has the secondary accent.

	Number of Syllables	Syllable with Primary Accent	Syllable with Secondary Accent
1. midnight			
2. contribution			
3. grapevine			
4. independence			
5. disappointment			
6. underneath			
7. naturalize			

In each row, circle the words that contain the sound shown at the beginning of the row.

1. **k**	chant	panic	chorus	license	sincere
2. **s**	celery	sure	propose	pounce	satin
3. **sh**	social	fiction	mission	parachute	pursue
4. **ch**	culture	machine	grouch	question	anchor
5. **d**	product	ideal	graduate	doom	ledge
6. **j**	genius	dodge	gum	reduce	schedule
7. **g**	image	agent	disguise	gem	gear
8. **z**	raisin	verse	lose	pajamas	sandal
9. **zh**	nation	casual	assure	basic	vision
10. **t**	granite	clothing	ditch	item	fourteen
11. **th**	smother	thaw	northern	theory	faith
12. **th**	there	method	lather	thirst	rhythm
13. **ks**	anxious	wax	exact	expense	index
14. **gz**	exist	mix	exhaust	extreme	next
15. **y**	type	youth	glory	yarn	beyond
16. **w**	awake	fawn	dew	bewilder	wasp

Divide each word below into syllables.

1. local

2. subtract

3. double

4. summon

5. hamster

6. joyous

7. armor

8. poet

9. flagpole

10. sandal

11. petal

12. rumble

13. missile

14. method

15. dial

In each row, circle the words that contain the same vowel sound.

1. sweat   cease   grief   search   seize   bleed

2. dread   peg   pearl   gleam   lend   wedge

3. froze   mow   soul   cloak   pouch   due

4. plaid   brace   drain   steak   bay   prey

5. bluff   flood   rough   pounce   hunch   lurk

6. scowl   tough   sprout   towel   bough   crow

7. few   stew   crowd   cube   hook   cute

8. mare   charm   sheer   arc   yarn   moor

9. bruise   book   hood   pew   foul   brook

10. purr   bear   fir   earth   ford   work

11. fare   shear   learn   gear   hire   nor

12. pure   chore   pierce   wore   harm   worse

13. caw   doubt   jog   chalk   ought   sauce

14. bond   cork   choice   oat   sock   lodge

15. brood   took   chute   dew   blood   rove

16. employ   scow   avoid   heroic   spoil   soul

17. wear   lose   dare   smear   chore   worst

18. bribe   tie   sly   brief   they   knight

A contraction is made from two or more words. An apostrophe (') represents the letter or letters that have been left out.

On the first line after each pair of words, write their contraction. On the second line, write the letter or letters that have been left out.

1. had not _____ _____
2. you have _____ _____
3. would not _____ _____
4. I am _____ _____
5. he is _____ _____
6. there has _____ _____

7. you will _____ _____
8. what has _____ _____
9. where is _____ _____
10. we shall _____ _____
11. do not _____ _____
12. we had _____ _____

Write the words that formed each of these contractions.

1. here's _____
2. you'd _____
3. she's _____
4. he'll _____
5. you're _____
6. he'd _____

7. we've _____
8. that's _____
9. shouldn't _____
10. she'll _____
11. we're _____
12. hasn't _____

Some contractions have two meanings. For example, *I'd* may mean *I had* or *I would*. The meaning of the sentence tells which words *I'd* stands for.

The contraction in front of each sentence below has two meanings. Complete the sentence by writing on each line the two correct words represented by the contraction.

she's   1. _____ usually been prompt, but _____ late today.

they'd   2. _____ have been hurt, but _____ buckled their seat belts.

she'd   3. If _____ had enough gasoline, _____ have finished the lawn.

where's   4. _____ Nita been, and _____ she now?

A compound word is formed by joining two or more small words.

Join one word from each list to make compound words. Write the compound words on the lines.

new	made	1. _____
barber	born	2. _____
home	bee	3. _____
tooth	pick	4. _____
sand	shop	5. _____
winter	soil	6. _____
bumble	paper	7. _____
top	time	8. _____

Sometimes a compound word is written as one word, sometimes as separate words, and sometimes with a hyphen connecting the small words.

flagpole   *telephone book*   *soft-boiled*

Circle the compound word in each sentence below. Then write its separate parts on the line in front of the sentence.

_____ 1. At dawn we rolled up our sleeping bags, packed our gear, and started to hike.

_____ 2. Although the old bulldog looked mean, it was really quite friendly.

_____ 3. Have you ever seen a flying saucer?

_____ 4. Todd's family visited a sawmill to see how trees are cut into boards.

_____ 5. There's Mr. Sanchez washing his brand-new car.

_____ 6. The second baseman grabbed the ball, turned, and threw out the runner.

_____ 7. After Tina left the store, she realized that she had been shortchanged by $5.00.

_____ 8. Mike began sneezing just a few minutes after entering the air-conditioned room.

_____ 9. Nicole used her first-aid training to treat my burn.

Plurals are words that name more than one. They are formed in several ways.

1 Add -s to most words.

sock—socks

2 Add -es to words that end in s, x, sh, ch, or tch.

loss—losses   bush—bushes
tax—taxes   couch—couches
stitch—stitches

3 Change y to i and add -es to words that end in a consonant plus y.

diary—diaries

4 Add -s to words that end in a vowel plus y.

monkey—monkeys

5 Change f to v and add -s or -es to words that end in f or fe.

calf—calves   life—lives

6 If a word ends in a consonant plus o, usually -es is added. If it ends in a vowel plus o, usually -s is added.

hero—heroes   cuckoo—cuckoos

On the first line after each word below, write the number of the sentence above that tells how to form its plural. On the second line, write the plural form.

1. injury _____ _____
2. lens _____ _____
3. dingo _____ _____
4. ax _____ _____
5. loaf _____ _____
6. activity _____ _____
7. match _____ _____

8. runway _____ _____
9. gash _____ _____
10. pouch _____ _____
11. studio _____ _____
12. igloo _____ _____
13. stack _____ _____
14. knife _____ _____

Some plurals are formed by changing one or more letters within the word, as in *mouse—mice*. Some plural forms are spelled the same as the singular, as in *deer—deer.*

Write the plural form of each word below. Use a dictionary if necessary.

1. tooth _____
2. sheep _____
3. woman _____
4. goose _____

5. foot _____
6. moose _____
7. trout _____
8. man _____

The possessive form of a word shows ownership.

1 Add *'s* to words that name one person or animal.	**2** Add an apostrophe (*'*) to plural words that end in *s*.	**3** Add *'s* to plural words that do not end in *s*.
an artist's brush	*the knights' armor*	*the mice's tails*

Complete each sentence below with the possessive form of one of the following phrases. Then on the line in front of the sentence, write the number of the sentence above that tells how to make the phrase possessive.

ears of doe	choice of people	rights of citizens
hump of camel	strength of oxen	den of cougar
ships of admirals		training of police officers

____ 1. It was the _____ that brought many pioneers across the Rockies.

____ 2. Everyone stayed up late on election night to see who would be the

_____.

____ 3. The United States Constitution clearly sets forth _____.

____ 4. Does a _____ really store water for long periods of time?

____ 5. _____ covers many methods of crime prevention.

____ 6. The _____ was a well-hidden cave near the top of the mountain.

____ 7. When she heard the crackling twig, the _____ perked straight up.

____ 8. _____ are called flagships because they fly special flags.

The spelling of some words is not changed when a suffix is added.

goal + s = goals   thaw + ing = thawing   chalk + y = chalky
tax + es = taxes   broad + er = broader   brief + ly = briefly
soak + ed = soaked   harsh + est = harshest   grace + ful = graceful

Rewrite each word below, adding the ending above the column.

s

rib _____

wasp _____

ski _____

es

smash _____

peach _____

ditch _____

ed

raid _____

cash _____

loan _____

ing

bleed _____

clang _____

moo _____

er

strict _____

rough _____

mild _____

est

bold _____

tall _____

weak _____

y

fuzz _____

grouch _____

salt _____

ly

saint _____

rare _____

strong _____

ful

peace _____

dread _____

joy _____

In each sentence below, underline the word whose spelling was not changed before the suffix was added. Then write its base word on the line in front of the sentence.

_____ 1. After the storm, the beach town was a sorrowful mess.

_____ 2. To buy Boardwalk was risky, but the move won the game for Allison.

_____ 3. For Thanksgiving, we chose the plumpest turkey in the store.

_____ 4. Why do compasses always point to the north?

_____ 5. Very few people have attempted to climb Mt. Everest.

_____ 6. Our muddy little puppy crept timidly in the door.

In some words, the final consonant is doubled before a suffix is added.

jab + b + ed = jabbed   blur + r + y = blurry
slit + t + ing = slitting   jog + g + er = jogger

Rewrite each word below, adding the ending above the column. Remember to double the final consonant.

ed

chug _____

outwit _____

prefer _____

stun _____

ing

brag _____

permit _____

throb _____

occur _____

y

scrap _____

mud _____

fog _____

er

skip _____

blot _____

win _____

In each sentence below, underline the word in which the final consonant was doubled before the suffix was added. Then write its base word on the line in front of the sentence.

_____ 1. One of the bridges spanning San Francisco Bay is called the Golden Gate.

_____ 2. The hot weather and smoggy air made everyone feel uncomfortable.

_____ 3. Patrolling the streets at night can be lonely for a police officer.

_____ 4. You look slimmer today than the last time I saw you.

_____ 5. The *Titanic* rammed an iceberg and sank quickly.

_____ 6. Kevin is a long-distance runner on the track team.

_____ 7. Taylor's job was shredding the lettuce for the tacos.

_____ 8. Ms. Tyson jotted our homework assignment on the chalkboard.

In most words that end in a consonant plus *y*, the *y* is changed to *i* before a suffix is added.

$$gupp\cancel{y} + i + es = guppies \qquad wear\cancel{y} + i + est = weariest$$
$$appl\cancel{y} + i + ed = applied \qquad eas\cancel{y} + i + ly = easily$$
$$tid\cancel{y} + i + er = tidier \qquad fanc\cancel{y} + i + ful = fanciful$$

Rewrite each word below, adding the ending above the column. Remember to change the *y* to *i*.

es		**ed**		**er**	
activity	_____	horrify	_____	friendly	_____
bully	_____	petrify	_____	stony	_____
melody	_____	shy	_____	shady	_____
daisy	_____	deny	_____	bulky	_____

est		**ly**		**ful**	
husky	_____	angry	_____	plenty	_____
soggy	_____	happy	_____	mercy	_____
tiny	_____	pretty	_____	bounty	_____
tricky	_____	hungry	_____	beauty	_____

In each sentence below, underline the word in which the *y* was changed to *i* before the suffix was added. Then write its base word on the line in front of the sentence.

_____ 1. The old boat ferried cars across the river one last time.

_____ 2. One of Crazy Horse's greatest victories occurred at Little Bighorn.

_____ 3. The telescope magnified Venus so that I could see it clearly.

_____ 4. The fuzziest puppy was also the smallest.

_____ 5. As the sun set, the sky turned beautiful shades of violet.

_____ 6. The movers left the bulkiest cartons until last.

_____ 7. After the long game, Pat trudged wearily home.

_____ 8. The road was temporarily closed for repairs.

In most words that end in silent e, the e is dropped before a suffix is added.

trace + ed = traced   dense + er = denser   grease + y = greasy
dodge + ing = dodging   fierce + est = fiercest   piece + es = pieces

Rewrite each word below, adding the ending above the column. Remember to drop the final silent e.

	ed		**ing**		**er**
advance	_____	rinse	_____	vote	_____
wriggle	_____	brace	_____	slice	_____
scrape	_____	grope	_____	hike	_____
pierce	_____	wheeze	_____	voyage	_____

	est		**y**		**s**
brave	_____	ice	_____	face	_____
severe	_____	double	_____	tease	_____
strange	_____	injure	_____	phrase	_____
tense	_____	miserable	_____	dice	_____

In each sentence below, underline the word in which the final silent e was dropped before the suffix was added. Then write its base word on the line in front of the sentence.

_____ 1. Veronica has the tamest parakeet I've ever seen.

_____ 2. Although the puzzle looked simple, it was quite baffling.

_____ 3. What is the largest city in the United States?

_____ 4. The mayor is advising everyone to stay indoors during the storm.

_____ 5. The relay races start in an hour.

_____ 6. The dry pine logs crackled as they burned.

_____ 7. All week long the weather was hot and hazy.

_____ 8. The quarterback avoided a tackler and passed the football.

1	The spelling of some words is not changed before a suffix is added, as in *bats*.	3	In words that end in a consonant plus *y*, the *y* is changed to *i* before a suffix is added, as in *happier*.
2	In some words, the final consonant is doubled before a suffix is added, as in *nutty*.	4	In most words with a final silent *e*, the *e* is dropped before a suffix is added, as in *coming*.

On the first line in front of each word below, write the number of the sentence above that tells how the suffix was added. On the second line, write the base word.

___	_____	1. widest	___ _____	21. organizer
___	_____	2. slowly	___ _____	22. actively
___	_____	3. racer	___ _____	23. fanciful
___	_____	4. surfing	___ _____	24. controlling
___	_____	5. hurtled	___ _____	25. satisfied
___	_____	6. witty	___ _____	26. baker
___	_____	7. cities	___ _____	27. raffling
___	_____	8. answered	___ _____	28. thinner
___	_____	9. palest	___ _____	29. calamities
___	_____	10. dancing	___ _____	30. rinks
___	_____	11. gritty	___ _____	31. merrily
___	_____	12. plentiful	___ _____	32. loved
___	_____	13. greasy	___ _____	33. teary
___	_____	14. wonderful	___ _____	34. contrarily
___	_____	15. bulkiest	___ _____	35. coldest
___	_____	16. runner	___ _____	36. probably
___	_____	17. rehearses	___ _____	37. batted
___	_____	18. tagged	___ _____	38. smoky
___	_____	19. longer	___ _____	39. cared
___	_____	20. fretting	___ _____	40. glasses

The prefixes *in-*, *non-*, *dis-*, and *un-* mean "not."

in | direct   non | stop
dis | like   un | known

If a word begins with *m, b,* or *p,* the spelling of *in-* is generally changed to *im-,* as in *impure.*

The prefixes *un-* and *dis-* can also mean "the opposite of" the word to which they are added, as in *unlock* and *disappear.*

The prefix *mis-* means "wrong," as in *misspell.*

Underline the prefix in each word below. Then write the base word.

1. nonliving _____   4. misplace _____

2. disconnect _____   5. uncover _____

3. incomplete _____   6. immature _____

Complete the paragraph below by adding *in-, im-, non-, dis-, un-,* or *mis-* to the word given below each line. Use a dictionary if necessary.

Today was one of those _____ days. I felt completely
                                                    (possible)

_____. Should I move to another planet? At first it seemed
        (human)

_____ which one. Then I realized that I had _____.
        (important)   (judged)

I had to _____ Mercury as too close to the sun. Our neighbor
                    (regard)

Venus seemed _____ with all its poisonous gases. A trip to lifeless
                        (friendly)

Mars would be a _____. The giants Jupiter and Saturn are
                            (adventure)

_____ balls of gas. _____ and cold best describe
        (agreeable)   (Active)

Uranus and Neptune. And visitors would appear _____ on the
                                                                    (frequently)

"dwarf planet," Pluto. I finally decided it's all right to be right here for now, even

if Earth is _____.
                    (perfect)

The prefix *pre-* means "before."	The prefix *inter-* means "between" or "among."
pre l *cooked*	*inter* l *collegiate*
The prefix *bi-* means "two."	The prefix *tri-* means "three."
bi l *cycle*	*tri* l *angle*

Underline the prefix in each word below. Write the base word.

1. tricolor _____

2. interact _____

3. bicuspid _____

4. interlock _____

5. prefix _____

6. tricycle _____

7. biplane _____

8. prearrange _____

In some words, when the prefix is taken away, the part that is left is not a familiar word, as in *interfere* and *predict*. But the meaning of the prefix may help in defining the whole word. Sometimes it is necessary to use a dictionary.

Underline the word with the prefix *pre-, inter-, bi-,* or *tri-* in each sentence below. Draw a line after the prefix. Then write the definition of the word containing the prefix. Use a dictionary if necessary.

1. Traces of prehistoric people have been found throughout the world.

_____

2. Casey used binoculars to watch the many birds stopping at Hawk Mountain.

_____

3. Planes from many different countries land at international airports.

_____

4. I get very angry when Dana interrupts my conversations.

_____

5. We saw the preview of a pirate movie that opens next week.

_____

6. Our club has a bimonthly newspaper collection drive to help save trees.

_____

The prefix *re-* means "back" or "again." re | place re | count	The prefix *super-* means "more than" or "above." super | highway
The prefix *fore-* means "in front." fore | head	The prefix *sub-* means "under" or "below." sub | title

Underline the prefix in each word below. Write the base word.

1. superpower _____
2. subcommittee _____
3. forepaw _____
4. refuel _____
5. reappear _____
6. foresee _____

7. superstar _____
8. forethought _____
9. subtopic _____
10. subnormal _____
11. recall _____
12. supernatural _____

Underline the word with the prefix *re-*, *super-*, *fore-*, or *sub-* in each sentence below. Draw a line after the prefix. Then write the definition of the word containing the prefix. Use a dictionary if necessary.

1. Both Baltimore and Washington have good subway systems.

   _____

2. Pat put the car in reverse to get out of the parking space.

   _____

3. An old, weathered barn stood in the foreground of the picture.

   _____

4. To earn spending money, my sister works at a supermarket.

   _____

5. Supersonic jets cross the Atlantic Ocean in just a few hours.

   _____

6. The rain became so heavy that the hikers had to return to camp.

   _____

The prefixes *over-*, *under-*, *up-*, *down-*, *in-*, and *out-* often show position or direction.

over | head   under | ground   up | stairs
down | stairs   in | doors   out | doors

Complete the paragraphs below by adding *over-*, *under-*, *up-*, *down-*, *in-*, or *out-* to the word given below each line.

Believe it or not, a Copperhead Snake Roundup is held yearly in the woods and

_____ _____ York, Pennsylvania. I went last summer. It
    (brush)   (side)

was a perfect day to be _____. Walking _____ along a
                              (doors)   (stream)

river, I looked carefully under the rocks. After a while, I moved _____
                                                                        (land)

from the river. I walked _____ to a high rock that _____ a
                              (hill)   (looks)

large wooded area. There I spotted a lumber pile that might be a likely place to find

a copperhead. So I started to walk back _____. I didn't have to worry
                                              (hill)

about being _____ or _____ from snakes. They don't have
                  (wind)   (wind)

a good sense of smell. But they can feel movement coming _____
                                                                (land)

toward them. As I got closer, I was almost walking on my tiptoes. Suddenly I saw it.

Curled _____ the pile of lumber was a copperhead. I caught it with a
            (side)

special rod used for hunting poisonous snakes. I'm glad I didn't spend that day

_____. The Roundup was great, even though I had to watch carefully
    (doors)

for what was _____.
                  (foot)

The suffixes *-ion*, *-sion*, *-ation*, and *-ition* mean "the action of doing" or "the state of being."

direction   adoration

The suffixes *-able* and *-ible* mean "able to" and "able to be."

avoidable   responsible

Underline the suffix in each word below. Then write the base word. Use a dictionary to check the spelling if necessary.

1. relaxation _____

2. reversible _____

3. protection _____

4. returnable _____

5. repetition _____

6. payable _____

Complete the paragraph below by adding *-ion*, *-sion*, *-ation*, *-ition*, *-able*, or *-ible* to the word given below each line. Use a dictionary if necessary.

When we moved to our farm, the barn was old and in great

_____. During a close _____, Dad found a lot
(confuse)   (inspect)

of metal. My first _____ was that he had found trash. But Dad's
(react)

_____ of the pile was "scrap." His _____ was
(define)   (explain)

that we would recycle it. "We'll be making a _____ to
(contribute)

the environment," he said. The different kinds of metal weren't

_____ to me, but Dad knew them. The _____
(recognize)   (sense)

thing to do was to put them in different piles. Our _____ was
(conclude)

that we could get money for the metal from a scrap yard.

The suffix -ful means		The suffix -less means	
"full of"	_hopeful_	"without"	_endless_
"the amount that fills"	_armful_		
The suffix -y means		The suffix -ly means	
"like"	_chummy_	"like"	_friendly_
"full of"	_rocky_	"each" or "every"	_nightly_
"the state of being"	_honesty_	"in a way that is"	_quietly_

Complete the paragraphs below by writing *-ful, -less, -y,* or *-ly* on each line.
Use a dictionary if necessary.

Crater Lake is clear, deep, and peace_____. From a distance it almost

seems motion_____. It hasn't aways been that way, though. Crater Lake

was born violent_____. A volcano called Mazama once stood in its place.

One day, it complete_____ blew its top, tossing out much more than just a

hand_____ of stones. It showered a dust_____ coat of ashes, rock, and lava

over Oregon and much of Canada. The explosion was so power_____ that it

collapsed the top of the mountain. Then this giant opening slow_____ filled

with rain. After thousands of years, just a cup_____ at a time, Crater Lake

was formed.

Mazama was one of the volcanoes in the Ring of Fire. This is a world-sized

arm_____ of volcanoes. It stretches around the salt_____ coastlines of the

Pacific Ocean. It runs from the snow_____ peaks of South America to the

wind_____ islands of Alaska. It has over 600 volcanoes. Some have rested

silent_____ for many years. Others have made fright_____ shows of hot

lava and flame.

Write each word from the paragraph that ends with the suffix *-ful* in the correct column.

"full of"	"the amount that fills"

_____ _____ _____ _____

_____ _____

The suffixes -er and -or mean "a person who."

reporter   *inventor*

The suffix -ist also means "a person who." It tells that the person has something to do with the base word, as in *scientist*.

Identify each person described below by adding -er, -or, or -ist to a word in the word box. Write the new word on the line. The spelling of the base word may have to change before the suffix is added. Use a dictionary if necessary.

WORD BOX

educate	astronomy	visit	buy
village	conduct	compose	colony
govern	drug	discover	help
collect	novel	inspect	motor

1. A person who purchases things   _____

2. A person who gives aid to another   _____

3. A person who sells medicines   _____

4. A person who lives in a small town   _____

5. A person who first finds a place or a thing   _____

6. A person elected to be the head of a state   _____

7. A person who teaches others   _____

8. A person who settles in a new land   _____

9. A person who writes music   _____

10. A person who carefully looks over things   _____

11. A person who drives a car   _____

12. A person who saves things such as stamps   _____

13. A person who is a guest   _____

14. A person who leads an orchestra   _____

15. A person who writes books   _____

16. A person who studies the sun, the stars, etc.   _____

The suffix *-al* has two meanings: "of or belonging to," as in *personal*, and "the action of," as in *arrival*.

The suffixes *-ish* and *-ous* mean "like," as in *clownish* and *disastrous*.

The suffix *-ish* also means "somewhat," as in *sickish*.

The suffixes *-ous* and *-ious* mean "full of," as in *humorous* and *gracious*.

Underline the suffix in each word below. Write the base word.

1. stylish _____

2. colonial _____

3. nervous _____

4. victorious _____

5. accidental _____

6. selfish _____

Complete the paragraphs below by adding *-al, -ish, -ous,* or *-ious* to the word given below each line. Use a dictionary if necessary.

For many years, the _____ dollar coin was the _____
(tradition)   (large)

silver dollar. Its _____ past was greatest in the olden days of the
(glory)

_____ Old West. Its size and weight made the nickname "cartwheel"
(prosper)

seem quite _____.
(nature)

But in modern times, the dollar coin has seen only _____ use.
(occasion)

_____ reasons have been given for this. For one thing, it's
(Vary)

_____ to carry a pocketful of heavy coins when we have paper money.
(fool)

In 1979, a new dollar coin was minted. It was _____ and
(small)

_____. The Susan B. Anthony coin was also _____ for
(experiment)   (historic)

another reason. It was the first U.S. coin to honor an American woman. Now a new

series of dollar coins has been minted. These coins honor the presidents of the

United States.

The suffixes -*ment*, -*ness*, -*hood*, and -*ship* mean "the state of being."

settle<u>ment</u>   happi<u>ness</u>   brother<u>hood</u>   friend<u>ship</u>

The suffix -*ment* also means "the action of doing," as in move<u>ment</u>, and "a thing that," as in punish<u>ment</u>.

The suffixes -*ward* and -*wards* mean "in the direction of," as in eas<u>tward</u> and back<u>wards</u>.

Underline the suffix in each word below. Write the base word.

1. membership _____

2. illness _____

3. homeward _____

4. statement _____

5. knighthood _____

6. upwards _____

Complete the paragraph below by adding -*ment*, -*ness*, -*hood*, -*ship*, -*ward*, or -*wards* to the word given below each line.

The giant hot air balloon began to lift gently _____. It
                                                              (sky)
was August 16, 1960. Captain Joseph W. Kittinger, Jr., was fulfilling a

_____ dream. In the _____ of the morning,
            (boy)   (still)
he rose steadily _____. The _____ free-fall
                              (up)   (champion)
parachute jump of all time was about to happen. The _____
                                                                    (bright)
of the sun struck Kittinger's eyes. Then he jumped _____ at
                                                                        (out)
12,800 feet. This was a _____ dream no longer. This was an
                                    (child)
_____. One hardship Kittinger faced was a temperature of
        (achieve)
-94°F. One reward was the _____ of the world's record.
                                        (owner)

Underline the prefixes and the suffixes in the words below. Then write the base words on the lines.

1. prepay _____

2. operator _____

3. blameless _____

4. interchange _____

5. sweetness _____

6. bluish _____

7. dishonest _____

8. skillful _____

9. retold _____

10. pavement _____

11. lumpy _____

12. permission _____

13. misfortune _____

14. undersea _____

15. mouthful _____

16. declaration _____

17. downhill _____

18. toaster _____

19. hazardous _____

20. northward _____

21. triangle _____

22. supermarket _____

23. definition _____

24. knighthood _____

25. partnership _____

26. immature _____

27. homewards _____

28. gracious _____

29. foretell _____

30. cultural _____

31. outdoor _____

32. artist _____

33. manageable _____

34. disorderly _____

35. subtropical _____

36. biweekly _____

37. indivisible _____

38. reaction _____

39. unevenly _____

40. bicyclist _____

41. disagreeable _____

42. nonpayment _____

In the paragraphs below, underline each word that has one of these prefixes or suffixes.

Prefixes: *in-, im-, non-, dis-, un-, mis-, pre-, inter-, bi-, tri-, re-, super-, fore-, sub-, over-, under-, up-, down-, in-, out-*

Suffixes: *-ion, -sion, -ation, -ition, -able, -ible, -ful, -less, -y, -ly, -er, -or, -ist, -al, -ish, -ous, -ious, -ment, -ness, -hood, -ship, -ward, -wards*

For an unknown number of centuries, people looked in quiet wonderment at the moon. Moonbeams were said to make people act in foolish ways or even cause madness. No one was truly sure what the moon was made of either. One fanciful tale claimed that it was green cheese.

Galileo was the first scientist to do any studious work concerning the moon. He used his new invention, the telescope, to look at it. He described what he saw as mountains and seas. Many people found it believable that the moon's seas were full of water. Some truthless stories also described small, greenish creatures living there. Others told of nonhuman beings with bat wings.

Finally, in 1969, many old questions were answered by *Apollo* 11. Two adventurous astronauts landed on the moon. Everyone had foreknowledge that there would be no sandy beaches or water. The astronauts learned a great deal, though. The moon is in the neighborhood of 4.6 billion years old. That's as old as the universe itself.

List the underlined words below. Write the base word for each one.

1. _____ _____

2. _____ _____

3. _____ _____

4. _____ _____

5. _____ _____

6. _____ _____

7. _____ _____

8. _____ _____

9. _____ _____

10. _____ _____

11. _____ _____

12. _____ _____

13. _____ _____

14. _____ _____

15. _____ _____

16. _____ _____

17. _____ _____

18. _____ _____

Often words include the same root words. Knowing the meaning of the root word may help in defining unfamiliar words that contain them. For instance, *port* means "to carry." So, something *portable* is "able to be carried."

The words in each group below contain the same root word, which is defined above the group. Notice that if the root word is at the end of a word, it may have an ending added to it. Underline the root word that is the same in each group.

"at a distance"	"self"	"sound"	"to write"
telephone	automobile	saxophone	photograph
television	autograph	microphone	paragraph
telescope	automatic	symphony	biography

Complete each sentence below with one of the words above.

1. The musician played mellow tunes on a gleaming, golden _____.

2. A _____ call from Seattle to Portland doesn't cost very much.

3. Eager to know more about Abraham Lincoln, Carlos read a _____ about him.

4. Smiling, the basketball star wrote his _____ on Pam's program.

5. Through the _____, Dr. Fein could see galaxies millions of light years away.

6. When Lee turned the key and pressed the gas pedal, the _____ cruised down the road.

7. The old _____ showed Keisha's great-grandfather as a young boy.

8. At the beginning of this _____, the music is very soft.

9. This _____ device answers the phone and takes a message for you while you are away.

10. I had to write a _____ to explain why I was late for class.

One way to develop vocabulary is to learn the meaning of root words. For example, the root word *aud* means "to hear."

> *auditorium*—a place where people hear a speech, play, etc.
> *audible*—able to be heard
> *inaudible*—not able to be heard

The words in each group below contain the same root word, which is defined above the group. Notice that not all root words are spelled exactly alike. Underline the root word that is the same in each group.

"to carry"	"many"	"star"	"to see"
transport	multiply	astronomy	visible
import	multitude	astronaut	vision
porter	multimillionaire	asterisk	visit

Complete each sentence below with one of the words above.

1. Enormous tankers _____ oil across the oceans.

2. The _____ left the spaceship to make some repairs.

3. In the summer, mosquitoes _____ until there are millions.

4. Ashley's _____ is so poor that she did not see her friend waving from the corner.

5. The _____ hurried to the elevator with the load of suitcases.

6. The names of new members are marked with an _____.

7. Clever Ahmad came up with a _____ of possible solutions to our problem.

8. Since England can't raise enough crops for its people, it has to _____ food.

9. In the dense fog, only nearby objects were _____.

10. Mr. Kane won the lottery and became a _____.

On each line below, write the contraction formed by the two words.

1. there is _____

2. he would _____

3. have not _____

4. you will _____

5. would not _____

6. she has _____

7. I had _____

8. they have _____

Draw a line to connect the words that form a compound word. Then write the new compound word on the line.

bean	time	1. _____
pig	stalk	2. _____
space	boat	3. _____
tug	tail	4. _____
main	craft	5. _____
dinner	land	6. _____

Write the plural form of each word below.

1. calf _____

2. pulley _____

3. deer _____

4. lily _____

5. bunch _____

6. mouse _____

7. raisin _____

8. radio _____

Rewrite each phrase to show possession.

1. the eyes of a flounder _____

2. the office of the foremen _____

3. the meeting of the astronomers _____

4. the horn of a unicorn _____

5. the hooves of the yearlings _____

6. the artwork of the children _____

1 The spelling of some words is not changed before a suffix is added.	3 In some words, the final *y* is changed to *i* before a suffix is added.
2 In some words, the final consonant is doubled before a suffix is added.	4 In most words with a final silent *e*, the *e* is dropped before a suffix is added.

On the line in front of each word, write the number of the sentence above that tells how the ending was added to the word. On the line after the word, write its base word.

____ 1. tallest _____   ____ 5. daisies _____

____ 2. stranger _____   ____ 6. furry _____

____ 3. skipped _____   ____ 7. briefly _____

____ 4. voted _____   ____ 8. easier _____

After each word, write its word parts in the correct column.

	Prefix	Root Word	Suffix
1. disagreement	_____	_____	_____
2. unnecessarily	_____	_____	_____
3. interviewer	_____	_____	_____
4. impassable	_____	_____	_____
5. inhumanly	_____	_____	_____
6. misinformation	_____	_____	_____
7. uncomfortable	_____	_____	_____
8. trimonthly	_____	_____	_____

Underline the word part that is the same in each group.

autograph	portable	television	phonics
phonograph	export	visa	xylophone
photograph	report	visual	telephone
biography	porter	visible	symphony
graphic	import	visit	microphone

In order to use a dictionary you must be able to alphabetize words. Sometimes the first two, three, or more letters of words are the same. You must find the first letter in each word that is different. Then you must put the words in alphabetical order according to those letters.

Number the words in each group in alphabetical order.

____ crumb

____ cricket

____ crystal

____ crease

____ crossroad

____ flake

____ flavor

____ flagpole

____ flash

____ flank

____ treated

____ treason

____ treasure

____ tread

____ treaty

____ another

____ announced

____ announcement

____ announcer

____ annual

Think of a dictionary as having three parts: front, middle, and back.

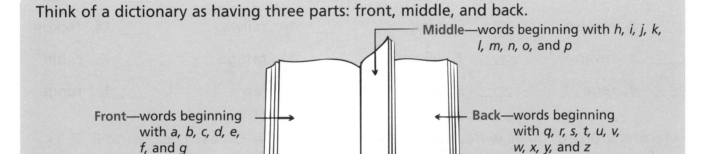

Middle—words beginning with h, i, j, k, l, m, n, o, and p

Front—words beginning with a, b, c, d, e, f, and g

Back—words beginning with q, r, s, t, u, v, w, x, y, and z

When you are looking for a word in a dictionary, decide which part it is in. Then open the dictionary to that part.

In which part of a dictionary are the following words found? On each line, write *front, middle,* or *back.*

1. ski _____

2. oat _____

3. bay _____

4. purr _____

5. hire _____

6. raid _____

7. vast _____

8. lily _____

9. gum _____

10. fuel _____

11. wow _____

12. den _____

The two words at the top of a dictionary page are called *guide words.* The one on the left tells the first word on the page. The one on the right tells the last word on the page. Words that come alphabetically between the two guide words are found on that page.

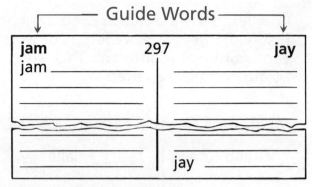

recall	420	regard	region	421	relieve

raft	418	ram	ramp	419	ray

Look at the guide words for the four dictionary pages shown above. On each line, write the number of the page on which the word is found.

____	1. relay	____	5. raid	____	9. rake	____	13. reliable
____	2. receive	____	6. rank	____	10. railway	____	14. reckon
____	3. raven	____	7. release	____	11. refuge	____	15. raisin
____	4. rage	____	8. reform	____	12. rap	____	16. range

Read the pair of guide words and the list of words below. On each line, write *B, O,* or *A* to indicate whether the word comes *before, on,* or *after* the page shown.

same	516	sardine

____	1. salmon	____	5. salute	____	9. satin	____	13. sample
____	2. satisfy	____	6. salad	____	10. saint	____	14. safety
____	3. sat	____	7. sandal	____	11. sandwich	____	15. sale
____	4. sameness	____	8. salt	____	12. sawdust	____	16. sandy

After each pair of guide words, write three words that would appear on that page.

1. **adopt—agree**   _____   _____   _____

2. **wedge—wheel**   _____   _____   _____

3. **poise—popular**   _____   _____   _____

4. **deck—dense**   _____   _____   _____

The words defined in a dictionary are called *entry words*. They are always listed alphabetically. Usually they are printed in dark type and divided into syllables.

Entry Word

Entry Word

dam¹ /dam/, **1.** a wall or barrier built to hold back any flowing water: *After the dam burst, many homes were flooded.* **2.** to provide with a dam: *Last summer we dammed the stream behind our house.* 1 *noun,* 2 *verb,* **dammed, dam•ming.**

dam² /dam/, a female parent, especially of four-footed animals, such as sheep, cattle, and horses. *noun.*

Dane /dān/, a person born or living in Denmark. *noun.*

Dix•ie /dik´sē/, the southern states of the United States, especially those that joined together to form the Confederacy. *noun.*

eer•ie or **eer•y** /ir´ē/, arousing fear because of strangeness; weird: *An eerie shadow crept slowly down the stairs.* *adjective,* **eer•i•er, eer•i•est.**

em•er•ald /em´ər əld/, **1.** a bright green precious stone. **2.** the color of an emerald. **3.** bright green. 1, 2 *noun,* 3 *adjective.*

faith•ful /fāth´fəl/, **1.** loyal; trustworthy; true: *The faithful dog was always at my side.* **2.** true to the facts; accurate: *This book gives a faithful account of that important event. adjective.* —**faith•ful•ly,** *adverb* —**faith•ful•ness,** *noun.*

fam•i•ly tree /fam´ə lē trē´/, a diagram that shows how the members of a family and their ancestors are related. *noun.*

fore•head /fôr´hed´ or fôr´id/, the part of the face above the eyes. *noun.*

for•syth•i•a /fôr sith´ē ə/, a bush that has many yellow bell-shaped flowers in the spring. *noun, plural* **for•syth•i•as.**

1. How many entry words are shown? _____

2. How many entry words begin with *e?* _____

3. How many entry words have only one syllable? _____

4. Which entry word has four syllables? _____

5. Which entry words begin with capital letters? _____

6. Which entry word has two words? _____

7. Which entry word has two spellings? _____

8. Which entry word has two pronunciations? _____

9. Which spelling has two entries? _____

10. Which entry word has a suffix? _____

If endings have been added to words, the words often are not listed as separate entry words. Instead, they are included within the entry of the root word.

ex•clude /ek slüd´/, to shut out; to keep out. *verb,* **ex•clud•ed, ex•clud•ing.**

grace•ful /grās´fəl/, showing beauty in form, movement, or manner; agreeable; pleasing: *The moves of the young dancer were very graceful. adjective.* —**grace•ful•ly,** adverb. —**grace•ful•ness,** *noun.*

The words below might not be listed as entry words in a dictionary. On the line after each one, write the entry word that would include it.

1. rarest _____

2. fascinating _____

3. tenderly _____

4. pressuring _____

5. jogged _____

6. lilies _____

7. valued _____

8. naughtier _____

9. horrified _____

10. yellowness _____

In each sentence below, underline the word that might not be listed as an entry word in a dictionary. Then above it, write the entry word that might include it.

1. Exercising on a regular basis is necessary to keep in good shape.

2. Does the sky seem bluer than usual today?

3. In its purest form, hydrogen is a very explosive gas.

4. The fog is always heavier at the airport than downtown.

5. The people of one country sometimes misunderstand the culture of other countries.

6. Did you see that car swing abruptly to the left and then run off the race track?

7. The largest animal in the world is the 100-foot-long blue whale.

8. By making oxygen, each plant and tree is a help to animal life.

If a word has more than one syllable, its entry word in a dictionary is divided into syllables. This division is shown either by a space or a heavy dot between the syllables.

ther mom e ter   or   **ther•mom•e•ter**

When writing a word, if it is necessary to divide it at the end of a line, divide it between syllables.

Find each of the following words in a dictionary. Rewrite it below, showing its syllables as given in the dictionary. Use a space or a heavy dot between the syllables.

meow	affectionate	quality	organization
literature	numeral	gratitude	dynamite
glorious	university	frantic	average
wrestle	satisfaction	variety	international
continent	triangle	blunder	knowledge
professional	institution	revolutionary	mechanical
zigzag	experimental	similar	huckleberry

1. _____

2. _____

3. _____

4. _____

5. _____

6. _____

7. _____

8. _____

9. _____

10. _____

11. _____

12. _____

13. _____

14. _____

15. _____

16. _____

17. _____

18. _____

19. _____

20. _____

21. _____

22. _____

23. _____

24. _____

25. _____

26. _____

27. _____

28. _____

In a dictionary, the pronunciation of each word is shown in parentheses after the entry word. The letters or symbols used represent the sounds heard in the word. The short pronunciation key below is like the one found in a dictionary.

Pronunciation Key

a	cat	ā	cake	ä	father	ch	chin	e	red		ē	see		ėr	her
g	get	i	big	ī	ride	j	jump	ng	ring		o	stop		ō	hope
ô	talk		oi	noise		ou	out		s	sit		sh	shall		th	thank
th	then		u	cut		u̇	put		ü	rule		ū	cute		zh	pleasure
ə	about, spoken, giraffe, police, picture							z	rose						

The paragraphs below contain eighteen numbered respellings. After the number of the word, write its correct spelling and the key word that tells how the underlined letter or letters are pronounced.

Nearly ¹ôl of the ²fif´tē states ³hav an official ⁴nik´nām´. Florida and South Dakota are ⁵bōth ⁶kôld the Sunshine State. New Jersey's nickname is the Garden State.

Most ⁷stāts have an official symbol, too. The symbol of Utah is the ⁸bē´hīv´. The official ⁹bėrd ¹⁰flī´ing in Iowa is the Eastern ¹¹gōld´finch´. The Rocky Mountain bighorn ¹²shēp is the official animal of Colorado. In Pennsylvania, ¹³fīr´flīz´ were ¹⁴kround the state ¹⁵in´sekt. Some states also have special ¹⁶trēz or flowers. New York's ¹⁷chois was the sugar maple, and Missouri's was the flowering ¹⁸dôg´wu̇d´ tree.

1. _____
2. _____
3. _____
4. _____
5. _____
6. _____
7. _____
8. _____
9. _____

10. _____
11. _____
12. _____
13. _____
14. _____
15. _____
16. _____
17. _____
18. _____

Every dictionary includes in its pronunciation key a symbol that looks like an upside down e /ə/. This symbol is called a *schwa*. It stands for the vowel sound often heard in an unaccented syllable. Each vowel can have the sound of the schwa, as in *zebra*, *siren*, *disease*, *bacon*, and *supply*.

In each word below, underline the vowel that stands for the schwa sound.

survive	rustier	telegram	leopard	barrier
errand	barrel	apricots	imagine	error
telegraph	civil	terrify	taller	terrific
subtract	servant	cactus	submarine	occurred
assured	tailor	rooster	armor	aside

On the line in front of each respelling below, write the vowel represented by the schwa. Then complete the crossword puzzle using the correct spelling of the word. Use the word list at the top of the page.

ACROSS

____ **1.** kak´təs
____ **5.** tə rif´ik
____ **8.** sər vīv´
____ **10.** lep´ərd
____ **11.** sub´mə rēn´
____ **13.** tā´lər
____ **14.** ə kėrd´
____ **15.** bar´e ər
____ **16.** ə sīd´

DOWN

____ **2.** ā´prə kots
____ **3.** er´ənd
____ **4.** siv´əl
____ **5.** tel´ə gram
____ **6.** rü´stər
____ **7.** i maj´ən
____ **8.** səb trakt´
____ **9.** ə shu̇rd´
____ **12.** är´mər

If a word has more than one syllable, sometimes more than one syllable is stressed. This is shown in a dictionary with a dark accent mark (´) placed after the syllable with the most stress. A light accent mark (´) is placed after the syllable that is also stressed but not as much.

vi´ o lin´   fire´ place´

Each word below is divided into syllables. Put a dark accent mark (´) after the syllable with the most stress. Put a light accent mark (´) after the syllable which is also stressed but not as much.

1. in tro duce
2. dem o crat ic
3. wa ter way
4. al li ga tor
5. co co nut
6. en er get ic
7. dan de li on

8. life like
9. u ni verse
10. sta tion ar y
11. kan ga roo
12. im i ta tion
13. rain bow
14. grand chil dren

15. cel e bra tion
16. tem po rar y
17. ac ci den tal
18. ge o graph ic
19. ex pe di tion
20. dis be lieve
21. in ter fer ence

On the line in front of each definition, write the correct word from the list above.

_____   1. An arch of color that is sometimes seen in the sky

_____   2. To make a person known to another

_____   3. A common weed with a yellow flower

_____   4. To think something is not true or real

_____   5. A large, hard-shelled fruit containing a white liquid

_____   6. Not planned; unexpected

_____   7. The activities for honoring a special occasion or person

_____   8. A mammal with strong hind legs for leaping

_____   9. A journey for a special purpose

_____   10. A large reptile similar to a crocodile

In a word with more than one syllable, usually at least one syllable is not stressed.

1 A syllable that contains the schwa sound is not stressed.

antlers
ant´ lərz

2 A syllable that is stressed is often followed by a syllable that is not stressed.

oriole
ôr´ ē ōl

3 A final syllable that is a consonant plus *le* is not usually stressed.

table
tā´ bəl

4 Prefixes and suffixes are usually not stressed.

catcher
kach´ ər

Each word below is divided into syllables. Put an accent mark after the syllable with the most stress. Then on the line in front of the word, write the number of the sentence above that tells about the unstressed syllable. (Sometimes more than one number can be used.)

_____ 1. cal en dar

_____ 2. treat ment

_____ 3. fum ble

_____ 4. un a ble

_____ 5. hol i day

_____ 6. le gal

_____ 7. ti tle

_____ 8. gov er nor

_____ 9. va ca tion

_____ 10. sau cer

_____ 11. peace ful

_____ 12. mel o dy

_____ 13. hus tle

_____ 14. pa ja mas

_____ 15. bee tle

_____ 16. ed u cate

_____ 17. in form

_____ 18. bu gle

_____ 19. dis play

_____ 20. joy ous

_____ 21. con quer

_____ 22. fa ble

_____ 23. sick ness

_____ 24. eld er

When the suffix *-al, -ial, -ic, -ical, -ion, -ation, -ian, -ious,* or *-ity* is added to a word, the primary accent shifts to the syllable before the suffix.

mem´ or y   me mo´ ri al   cur´ i ous   cur´ i os´ i ty

The shift of accent in a word with a suffix often results in a vowel change.

maj´ es ty (maj´ ə stē)   ma jes´ tic (mə jes´ tik)

Each word below is divided into syllables. Put a dark accent mark after the syllable with the most stress. Then circle any vowel that has a different sound when the suffix is added and the accent is shifted.

1. ad mire   ad mi ra tion   4. mag net   mag net ic
2. char ac ter   char ac ter is tic   5. her o   he ro ic
3. mu sic   mu si cian   6. col o ny   co lo ni al

Add one of the suffixes listed at the top of the page to the word below each line. Use a dictionary if you need spelling help.

The life of a farmer is filled with _____. Weather is always a
                                                (active)

key factor. Rainfall, sunshine, and _____ must occur in the proper
                                    (humid)

amounts and at the right times. Although the _____ farmer may
                                            (energy)

prefer to work in the sun, rainy days are a necessity, too. Nature is very

difficult to deal with. A sudden cold snap may wipe out the _____
                                                            (product)

of many months of labor. Another aspect of farming concerns the

_____ of the soil. The farmer must know the earth at the
    (fertile)

_____ and must work to make this earth produce. The farmer
    (locate)

must have talents, including the _____ of heavy machines and the
                                (operate)

_____ of fields. All of these things make farming an
    (irrigate)

_____ that provides great _____.
    (occupy)   (satisfy)

Sometimes a shift in accent changes the meaning of a word.

min•ute[1] (min′it), **1.** one-sixtieth of an hour; sixty seconds. **2.** a short time; an instant: *I'll do it in a minute. noun.*

mi•nute[2] (mī nüt′ *or* mī nyüt′), **1.** very small; tiny: *He has a minute speck of dirt in his eye.* **2.** concerning or paying attention to small details: *This paragraph contains a minute description of the child's face. adjective.* —**mi•nute•ly,** *adverb.* —**mi•nute•ness,** *noun.*

Pronounce each word in the word box. Then complete each sentence below by writing one of the word pairs on the lines. Divide the words into syllables and place the accent mark correctly.

—————————— **WORD BOX** ——————————

sub′ ject	con′ tent	per′ mit
sub ject′	con tent′	per mit′
up′ set	sus′ pect	des′ ert
up set′	sus pect′	de sert′

1. This _____ will _____ you to camp here for two days.

2. Do you _____ that the _____ will be caught?

3. After looking over the _____ of the book, I was quite _____ not to have read it.

4. Please do not _____ me to the _____ of Latin.

5. Robinson Crusoe and Friday did not _____ each other on the _____ island.

6. The basketball players were _____ when they lost in a last minute _____.

Pronunciation Key

a cat	ā cake	ä father	ch chin	e red	ē see	ėr her
g get	i big	ī ride	j jump	ng ring	o stop	ō hope
ô talk	oi noise	ou out	s sit	sh shall	th thank
th then	u cut	ů put	ü rule	ū cute	zh pleasure
ə about, spoken, giraffe, police, picture				z rose

Complete the paragraphs below by writing one of the following respellings on each line.

/mād/	/rōm/	/fä´thər/	/wůd/	/planz/	/moun´tənz/
/bôs/	/fū/	/trezh´ərz/	/trü´lē/	/trip/	/jum´bō/
/klīmd/	/shots/	/thrē/	/ėrth/	/chois/	/ə lông´/

Last year my _____ made a short business _____

to Africa. Not long before he left, his _____ said my mom and I

could go _____. For _____ weeks, we

_____ our preparations and _____. We had our

pictures taken for our passports. We also went to the doctor for the

_____ we _____ need.

Finally, the day arrived. We _____ aboard a huge

_____ jet plane. The flight across the Atlantic Ocean took only a

_____ hours.

Africa is _____ a beautiful continent. There are deserts, rain

forests, grassy plains, clear lakes, and snow-capped _____. Africa

has both large cities and tiny villages. Its _____ hides diamonds,

precious metals, and other _____. The most exciting animals in

the world _____ its forests and jungles. Best of all, the people's

friendliness made the trip a perfect one. If I had my _____, I'd

go back every year!

Pronunciation Key

a	cat	ā	cake	ä	father	ch	chin	e	red	ē	see	ėr	her
g	get	i	big	ī	ride	j	jump	ng	ring	o	stop	ō	hope
ô	talk	oi	noise	ou	out	s	sit			sh	shall	th	thank
th	then	u	cut	u̇	put	ü	rule			ū	cute	zh	pleasure
ə	about, spoken, giraffe, police, picture							z	rose		

On the first line in front of each definition below, write the respelling from the list.
On the second line, write the correct spelling. Use a dictionary if necessary.

/lath′ər/   /yung/   /pėr′chəs/   /gōt/   /shud′ər/
/ə fôrd′/   /lok′it/   /yärn/   /raft/   /pėr′sən/
/mezh′ər/   /jog/   /flint/   /meth′əd/   /hôr′nit/
/fling/   /ə void′/   /luk′out′/   /let′ər/   /glōb/

_____ _____ **1.** To find out the size or amount of something

_____ _____ **2.** Logs fastened together and used as a float

_____ _____ **3.** To buy

_____ _____ **4.** A large wasp

_____ _____ **5.** To keep away from

_____ _____ **6.** A person who watches

_____ _____ **7.** To shake from cold, fear, or horror

_____ _____ **8.** A way of doing something

_____ _____ **9.** To throw

_____ _____ **10.** Spun thread used for knitting

_____ _____ **11.** A round model of the earth

_____ _____ **12.** To run slowly

_____ _____ **13.** A foamy mixture of soap and water

_____ _____ **14.** To have the money for

_____ _____ **15.** Being in the early part of life

Most words have only one correct spelling. But some have more than one. In a dictionary, the alternate spellings are usually given before the respelling.

quar•tet or **quar•tette** /kwôr tet′/, **1.** a group of four singers or players. **2.** any group of four persons or things. *noun.*

The words below can be spelled correctly in more than one way. Find each word in a dictionary and write its alternate spelling on the line.

1. theater _____

2. marvelous _____

3. judgment _____

4. traveled _____

5. blond _____

6. skillful _____

7. nosy _____

9. ax _____

Many words have more than one correct pronunciation. All pronunciations that are correct are given in the respellings after the entry word.

frag•ile /fraj′əl/ /fra′ jīl′/ easy to break or damage; delicate. *adjective.*

The words below have more than one correct pronunciation. Find each word in a dictionary and write its alternate pronunciations on the lines.

1. vase _____ _____

2. route _____ _____

3. magazine _____ _____

4. pecan _____ _____

5. toward _____ _____

6. lasso _____ _____

7. neither _____ _____

8. pajamas _____ _____

9. tomato _____ _____

10. garage _____ _____

In a dictionary, some entry words also have illustrations. These pictures give additional help in explaining a word or a specific definition for a word.

a. casement

b. fiord

c. gondola

d. mustang

e. hatchet

f. hyena

g. partition

h. chamois

i. sloth

j. breakwater

k. sickle

l. dinghy

On the line in front of each definition below, write the letter of the picture it refers to.

____ **1.** A short-handled tool with a short, curved blade

____ **2.** A long, narrow boat

____ **3.** A large, wolflike animal

____ **4.** A window that opens on hinges

____ **5.** A small, goatlike antelope

____ **6.** A wall to protect a beach from the force of waves

____ **7.** A narrow bay between steep cliffs

____ **8.** A wall dividing a room into parts

____ **9.** A small, wild horse

____ **10.** A small rowboat

____ **11.** A small, short-handled ax

____ **12.** A slow-moving animal that hangs upside down from tree branches

Many words have more than one meaning. In the dictionary, each separate meaning is numbered.

Read the dictionary entries for *land* and *litter*. On the lines, write three sentences for each word. Use a different meaning in each sentence. On the line in front of the sentence, write the number of the meaning that is used in it.

land /land/, **1.** the solid part of the earth's surface: *After his first airplane flight, the man was glad to be on land again.* **2.** ground; soil: *This land is good for growing vegetables.* **3.** a country; a region; a farm: *Snowmobiles are not permitted on this land.* **4.** a nation: *People from many lands helped settle this country.* **5.** to come to the ground: *The pilot landed in Boston at 3 P.M.* **6.** to bring to the ground: *The pilot landed the plane in a field.* **7.** to go ashore from a boat: *The sailors landed at noontime.* **8.** to put ashore from a boat: *The ship landed the sailors.* 1–4 *noun,* 5–8 *verb.*

lit•ter /lit´ər/, **1.** things scattered around in disorder: *Clean up the litter before leaving the campsite.* **2.** the young animals born at one time: *Our dog had a litter of six puppies.* **3.** the material, such as straw, used as bedding for animals: *The farmhand placed fresh litter in each stall in the stable.* **4.** a stretcher for carrying a sick or wounded person: *They carried the injured player off the field on a litter.* **5.** a covered and usually curtained couch on a frame for carrying passengers: *The emperor was carried through the streets on a litter.* **6.** to leave things scattered about in disorder: *The crowds littered the street during the parade.* 1–5 *noun,* 6 *verb.*

Land

____ **1.** _____

_____

____ **2.** _____

_____

____ **3.** _____

_____

Litter

____ **1.** _____

_____

____ **2.** _____

_____

____ **3.** _____

_____

Many words have more than one meaning. In the dictionary, each separate meaning is numbered.

Complete each sentence below with a word from the word box. Then on the line below the sentence, write an original sentence showing another meaning for the word. Use a dictionary if necessary.

WORD BOX

yarn   organ   trip   stock   brand   square

1. The heart is the _____ that pumps blood through the body.

   _____

   _____

2. Columbus's first _____ across the Atlantic Ocean took several months.

   _____

   _____

3. To pass the evening hours, a pioneer might tell an interesting _____.

   _____

   _____

4. A difficult job for a cowhand was to _____ cattle out on the range.

   _____

   _____

5. In early America, the town _____ was often used as a meeting place.

   _____

   _____

6. The price of _____ in the company rose by three dollars a share.

   _____

   _____

Homographs are words that are spelled alike but have different meanings. Sometimes they are pronounced differently. In a dictionary, homographs are listed as separate entry words, each with a small number placed after it.

bat•ter[1] /bat´ər/, to strike with repeated blows; to pound; to beat violently. *verb.*

bat•ter[2] /bat´ər/, a thin liquid mixture of flour, milk, etc., used to make cakes, pancakes, etc. *noun.*

bat•ter[3] /bat´ər/, a person whose turn it is to bat in games like baseball. *noun.*

On the line in front of each sentence, write the number of the homograph used in that sentence. Then write an original sentence for the same homograph.

____ 1. After we stirred the blueberries into the batter, we put the pan in the oven.

_____

____ 2. The fourth batter in a baseball lineup is called the "cleanup" hitter.

_____

____ 3. The firefighters had to batter down the door to save the family.

_____

Each word in the word box is a homograph with two different meanings. Write the correct word on the line above each pair of definitions.

_____ **WORD BOX** _____

| prune | scale | loaf | mold | lap | firm |

1. _____
   a. One time around a race track
   b. To lick up with the tongue

2. _____
   a. A dried, sweet plum
   b. To trim trees

3. _____
   a. Strong; solid; hard
   b. A business company

4. _____
   a. A large piece of shaped bread
   b. To spend time doing nothing

5. _____
   a. A series of tones in music
   b. An instrument for weighing

6. _____
   a. To make into a form or shape
   b. A furry growth that appears on bread

Homophones are words that sound alike but are spelled differently and have different meanings.

> **flea** /flē/ a small, wingless jumping insect that lives in the fur of animals. *noun.*

> **flee** /flē/ **1.** to run away: *The cat will flee at the sound of the garbage truck.* **2.** to run away from: *The small children had to flee the loose dog.* **3.** to move quickly. *verb*, **fled, flee•ing.**

After each definition below, write the correct word from the word box.

WORD BOX

role	their	for	weigh	to
roll	there	four	way	two
won	meet	no	main	wood
one	meat	know	mane	would

1. Important _____
2. A part in a play _____
3. Two plus two _____
4. To understand _____
5. Succeeded _____

6. Belonging to them _____
7. The direction to go _____
8. One more than one _____
9. Building material _____
10. To get together with _____

Complete the paragraphs by writing homophones from the word box on the lines.

_____ day in November, _____ people in Boston took on a challenge. What was the fastest _____ to get to _____ jobs downtown? They decided to _____ at a supermarket parking lot. At five minutes before seven, they all started. One drove to a ferryboat dock; he found a parking space, and soon he was sitting on the boat. Another went to the new train station and parked his car; he got a seat and sat down to read his paper. The third commuter decided to drive to Boston. The traffic was already bumper-_____-bumper. And the last person drove to the closest commuter rail—where _____ was _____ place to park. He drove as fast as he could to the next rail stop, parked his car and hopped on. But he had to stand and hold on to the pole.

Who _____ you guess got _____ first? It wasn't the driver, who sat in traffic. And it wasn't the commuter on the crowded rail car. The train rider was sure he would win. But it was the commuter who took the ferryboat who _____ the race! He was at the finish 17 minutes before anyone else.

Synonyms are words that have the same, or almost the same, meaning.

Complete the paragraph below by writing a synonym from the word box for the word below each line.

WORD BOX

ideas	sickness	constructed	practical
hardships	select	errors	labor
fortunate	permitted	aid	neglect

Americans have always invented ways to _____ others. The
                                                    (help)

many _____ of our inventors have been turned into practical
          (thoughts)

items. They have _____ us to save time and _____ in
                      (allowed)   (work)

farming and industry. They have also helped to cure _____. Some
                                                         (illness)

of these inventions came about through _____. Others happened
                                             (mistakes)

after long hours of effort to overcome _____. Eli Whitney
                                            (difficulties)

_____ the first cotton gin in 1793. Robert Fulton put the first
     (built)

_____ steamboat in American waters in 1807. But the champion
     (useful)

inventor of the 1870s and 1880s was Thomas Edison. We're _____
                                                              (lucky)

he didn't _____ his ideas about electric lights, phonographs, and
                (ignore)

telegraphs. Now, _____ your favorite item and find out who first
                      (choose)

made it work.

Antonyms are words that are opposite in meaning.

Complete the paragraph below by writing an antonym from the word box for the word below each line.

WORD BOX

farthest	more	roundabout	noisy
quick	plentiful	daylight	common
find	alike	hotter	long

Many flocks of _____ geese stop at the Chesapeake Bay in
(silent)

Maryland during their trip south for the winter. The Chesapeake is an

important area for wildlife. While some birds travel a _____ way,
(short)

not all birds migrate. Those that travel south may do so to _____
(lose)

an area where food is more _____. Other reasons may include
(scarce)

_____ weather and longer hours of _____ in the
(colder)   (darkness)

South. The patterns of these birds are not _____. Some make
(different)

_____ migrations; others take _____ routes. Arctic
(slow)   (direct)

terns fly the _____ distance of all migrating birds. They move
(nearest)

from the Arctic to the Antarctic each year. That's a distance of

_____ than 20,000 miles a year! No matter where you live in the
(less)

United States, you can see migrating birds. Be on the watch next fall or

spring. You may see the _____ V-formation of ducks or geese.
(rare)

mag•ic /maj´ik/, **1.** the art of using claimed secret charms, spirits, supernatural powers, etc., to make unnatural things happen: *The wizard used magic to make the tree bear gold fruit.* **2.** anything that produces results in a secret way, as if by magic; an unexplained power or influence: *The magic of a parent's voice can calm down an upset child.* **3.** the skill of using the hand to complete clever tricks. **4.** done by magic or as if by magic: *He rode through the sky on a magic carpet.* 1–3 *noun,* 4 *adjective.*

ma•gi•cian (mə jish´ ən), **1.** a person skilled in magic. **2.** a person who entertains with magic tricks. *noun.*

man•u•fac•ture /man´ yə fak´ chər/, **1.** the making of products by hand or by machine, especially in large quantities. **2.** to make products by machine or by hand: *This factory manufactures children's clothing.* **3.** to make something into a useful form: *to manufacture rubber into tires.* **4.** to make up; to invent: *The poor sport manufactured reasons for losing the match.* 1 *noun,* 2–4 *verb,* **man•u•fac•tured, man•u•fac•tur•ing.**

mite[1] /mīt/, a very tiny animal that is similar to a spider and often lives in food and on plants and other animals. *noun.*

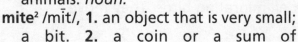

mite[2] /mīt/, **1.** an object that is very small; a bit. **2.** a coin or a sum of money with little value. **3.** a very small child. *noun.*

nar•ra•tor /nar´ā tər *or* na rā´tər/, a person who tells a story, *noun.*

neigh /nā/, **1.** the long, loud sound that a horse makes. **2.** to make this long, loud sound. 1 *noun,* 2 *verb.*

no•ti•fy /nō´ tə fī/, to give notice to someone; to make known; to inform; to announce to: *I will notify you if the meeting is postponed. verb,* **no•ti•fied, no•ti•fy•ing.**

No•vem•ber /nō vem´ bər/, the eleventh month of the year, having thirty days; the month just after October and just before December. *noun.*

o•be•di•ent /ō bē´ dē ənt/, willing to obey; doing what one is told; inclined to mind: *Very few cats are obedient. adjective.* —**o•be•di•ent•ly,** *adverb.*

o•ce•lot /ō´sə lot *or* os´ə lot/, a small, spotted wildcat found in Texas, Mexico, and parts of South America. *noun.*

oc•tet /ok tet´/, **1.** a piece of music for eight instruments or voices. **2.** a group of eight performers: *She plays the violin in a string octet.* **3.** any group of eight. *noun.*

ol•ive oil /ol´iv oil/, an oil pressed from olives and used in cooking, medicine, etc. *noun.*

om•e•let *or* **om•e•lette** /om´lit/, eggs beaten with milk or water, fried or baked, and folded over. *noun.*

Pronunciation Key

a	cat	ā	cake	ä	father	ch	chin	e	red		ē	see		ėr	her
g	get	i	big	ī	ride		j	jump		ng	ring	o	stop	ō	hope
ô	talk		oi	noise	ou	out		s	sit		sh	shall		th	thank
th	then	u	cut	u̇	put		ü	rule		ū	cute		zh	pleasure
ə	about, spoken, giraffe, police, picture									z	rose				

Use the sample dictionary page on page 74 to answer each question below.

1. What are the guide words on the sample dictionary page? _____

2. Write four words that would come before this page.

   _____

3. Write four words that would come after this page.

   _____

4. How many entry words are shown? _____

5. Which spelling has two entries? _____

6. Which entry words begin with *n?* _____

   _____

7. Which entry words have only one syllable? _____

8. Which entry words have four syllables? _____

9. Which entry word begins with a capital letter?_____

10. Which entry word has two words? _____

11. Which entry word has two spellings? _____

12. Which entry word names something that has whiskers? _____

13. Which entry words have two pronunciations? _____

14. Write two entry words with suffixes. _____

15. Under which entry word is *manufacturing* given? _____

16. Which entry words have more than one definition? _____

   _____

17. Which entry word shows that when a suffix is added to a word, sometimes the

   accented syllable changes? _____

18. Which entry word names something that has eight legs? _____

19. Which entry words contain the sound of the schwa? _____

   _____

20. Write a sentence for *manufacture* and the number of the definition used. _____

   _____

The words in slash marks show how a word is pronounced. On the lines, write the spelling for each word between slash marks.

1. I wonder if it will /snō/ /ôl/ day. _____ _____

2. D. J. never /thôt/ he /wůd/ win. _____ _____

3. May I have a /tūb/ of /tūth pāst/? _____ _____

4. We made sandwiches with /ōtmēl/ /bred/. _____ _____

5. The plane /klīmd/ to /thirtēn/ thousand feet. _____ _____

6. He solved the /puzəl/ through trial and /erər/. _____ _____

7. The /bābē/ /krīd/ all night. _____ _____

8. A new /brüm/ sweeps /klēn/. _____ _____

9. A /stich/ in time /sāvz/ nine. _____ _____

10. /menē/ hands make /līt/ work. _____ _____

Write a homophone, a word that sounds the same but is spelled differently, for each word below.

1. through _____

2. dew _____

3. brake _____

4. doe _____

5. route _____

6. flour _____

7. weigh _____

8. peace _____

9. night _____

10. plane _____

Circle the number of syllables in each word.

1. telephone   1   2   3   4

2. careless   1   2   3   4

3. breakfast   1   2   3   4

4. walked   1   2   3   4

5. interfere   1   2   3   4

6. edition   1   2   3   4

7. pitcher   1   2   3   4

8. absolutely   1   2   3   4

9. themes   1   2   3   4

10. intersection   1   2   3   4

Divide each word below into syllables and write it on the line. Then place an accent mark after the syllable that is stressed.

1. alphabet   _____

2. quarter   _____

3. interference   _____

4. contradiction   _____

5. number   _____

6. visible   _____

7. tunnel   _____

8. machine   _____

9. misplace   _____

10. joyful   _____

In each sentence, cross out two pairs of words. Then write the contraction for the words above each pair.

1. Tom said he is sick, but he does not have the flu.

2. I have eaten all of the grapes that were not rotten.

3. Who is going to tell us where we are supposed to meet?

4. If we had worked harder, we would be finished by now.

5. You are going to be late if you do not hurry up.

Write the plural form of each word on the line after the word.

1. battery _____   6. space _____

2. peach _____   7. cable _____

3. life _____   8. supply _____

4. article _____   9. hero _____

5. goose _____   10. tax _____

Write the possessive form of the first word on the line after the word.

1. doctor _____ office

2. nurses _____ shifts

3. watch _____ band

4. people _____ houses

5. mice _____ nests

On the lines at the right, write the prefix and suffix in each of the following words.

	Prefix	Suffix
1. uncomfortable	_____	_____
2. outsider	_____	_____
3. disagreement	_____	_____
4. international	_____	_____
5. prehistoric	_____	_____
6. reeducation	_____	_____
7. indivisible	_____	_____
8. nonhazardous	_____	_____
9. bimonthly	_____	_____
10. forenoonish	_____	_____

Change each of the words below to mean the opposite by adding one of these prefixes.

dis-   mis-   non-   un-   under-

1. nourished _____

2. pleasure _____

3. count _____

4. likely _____

5. fiction _____

Change each of the words below to an adjective by adding one of these suffixes.

-ful   -less   -ly   -ous   -y

1. cheer _____

2. neighbor _____

3. joy _____

4. care _____

5. mist _____

In each row, underline the synonym and circle the antonym of the first word.

1. **stern**   average   gentle   harsh   hungry

2. **false**   wild   vast   wrong   true

3. **bore**   drop   interest   tire   swell

4. **sensible**   foolish   dim   afraid   wise

5. **broad**   tall   wide   narrow   certain

6. **deny**   shrink   clean   refuse   grant

7. **linger**   save   hurry   fast   delay

8. **actual**   imaginary   real   confident   tame

9. **timid**   slow   bulky   bold   shy

10. **frequently** often   slowly   seldom   bitter

11. **permit**   forbid   watch   allow   break

12. **withdraw**   shine   retreat   tremble   advance

Using the root words and their meanings below, write a word to complete each sentence. Some words will include <u>two</u> root words.

aud "to hear"	**visi** "to see"	**graph** "to write"	**port** "to carry"
phon "sound"	**photo** "light"	**multi** "many"	**tele** "distant"
auto "self"	**loc** "place"	**astro** "star"	**geo** "earth"

1. The sound of the news program was _____ _____ through the wall.

2. Reese carries his _____ bicycle on the subway.

3. Can you tell me the _____ of the new shopping center?

4. If you use the _____ when you are on stage, everyone will be able to hear you.

5. The study of stars and planets is called _____.

6. A _____ choice question has several answer choices.

7. The author signed her _____ on the book I bought.

8. Our family likes to watch sports programs on _____.